do THAT thing

#gobegreat!

Angela S. Gailliard

Ayesghee Publishing

Allow yourself to be great, my friend.

Allow yourself to be great, my friend.

do THAT thing

#gobegreat!

Preface

I must admit. I have spent a lot of years doing "stuff". You know what I mean. Stuff. Unfruitful stuff. Stupid Stuff. "Stuff" that you really have no substantial reason for why you're doing it. "Stuff" that other people do that looks good to you and you think you should do it too. "Stuff" you think will get you to your ultimate destination. Stuff. I was doing so much "stuff" that I even jokingly called myself a "Jane of all Trades". It sounded funny and I got a few laughs but it was not a joke. I was tired. I was overwhelmed. But worst of all, despite all of the "stuff" I was doing, I had really just done much of nothing. There, I said it. I was doing things that probably would have amounted to a big deal had I had a process or a real plan but I didn't. My life resembled that of a hamster running on its wheel. I was busy doing nothing. I was beginning to feel like a failure. It took me hitting a really low point in my life for me to realize that I NOT supposed to be that space and that I had everything I needed to pull myself up and get it right. I'd come to a point where I really just needed to take a moment (well, it actually turned out to be a few days) to analyze what was going on in my life. I couldn't label my bad decisions as youthful mistakes. I was well beyond the age of "official adulthood" (i.e., over 30 years old). I even explored the fact I came from a single parent home with no positive role models in my life but, to me, that would have been just another excuse. I simply took responsibility for my own actions and made a decision.

> *Alright, Angela.* (Yes, I talk to myself in third person sometimes.) *Over the years, you've gained a wealth of knowledge and have had so many experiences – some were good and some were not so good. You've made some powerful connections and have been afforded opportunities for growth beyond where you are now. Why haven't you utilized that knowledge and those opportunities to your full advantage? Why have you allowed fear, feelings of inferiority, and other "stupid" things to keep you from reaching your full potential? All that you've learned you've kept buried.*

The time had come for me to *do THAT thing*. If you're reading this book, it is time for YOU to *do THAT thing*. Trust yourself and your ideas. Believe you can and get to work. It is time to tap into your hidden treasure.

What thing is it that you want to do? Embark on a new career? Go for it. Start a business? Do it. Go back to college? Go. Take a year off and explore the world? Awesome! It doesn't matter what that thing is, if you can conceive it then it can become a reality for you. How, you wonder? Experience has taught me that in order to *do THAT thing,* there were five basic aspects that must be considered and implemented – (1) you have to trust yourself and your abilities, (2) be original but don't re-invent the wheel, (3) don't try to do everything by yourself, (4) believe that you can do it, and (5) make the conscious decision to give it all you've got and go for it.

do THAT thing: #gobegreat! is designed to help you trust your gifts and talents and to start doing. Use it to guide you through your transformation process. Read it for encouragement. Find the strength you need through the experiences I share. Note that this is a guide. YOU have to put in the work. YOU have to check fear at the door. YOU have to form the relationships. YOU have to believe that you can *do THAT thing.*

1

Trust Yourself

Trust yourself. You know more than you think you do.

Dr. Benjamin Spock

When I first embarked on what I call "my personal renaissance", I was reminded of a particular Bible parable. It speaks of a businessman who gave his servants certain responsibilities while he was to be gone on an extended trip. He gave each servant a certain amount of responsibility and expected a return on his investment by the time he returned. The businessman didn't expect the men do more with his investment than he knew they could handle. He was familiar with each man's ability. However, he did expect each man to trust himself and his individual talents enough to go out there and do something great. When he finally returned, he went to settle with the three men. Two of the three had done just what he expected. They doubled the man's investment. He was so impressed that he made them partners in his business. The third man, however, didn't quite live up to his perceived potential. He had been so afraid of making a mistake and disappointing the businessman that he did nothing with what he was given. He just stuck it somewhere and didn't touch it again until the businessman returned. Matthew 25:26-30 (NIV) goes on to tell us just how furious the businessman was. He even called the servant "lazy" and "wicked". He then instructed his business partners to take back the responsibilities given to the man who did nothing with them and give it to the one who risked the most. Wow!

Like the third servant, many of us suffer from what I consider to be one of life's greatest injustices – **doubt**. Doubt, a by-product of fear, is a detrimental element that robs you of your confidence and leaves you feeling uncertain about that thing you once were certain you could achieve. Doubt is a dream crusher. It's criminal. Don't succumb to it. Don't let doubt kill your dream.

> *Doubt kills more dreams than failure ever will.*
> **Karim Seddiki**

I'm telling you. Doubt can creep in and just mess you up. It happened to me with my very first business idea. I was young (around twenty-two years old, I believe). I was a dreamer and had always dreamed of being a business owner. At the time, I had just been discharged from the Navy and was a new mom. I wanted to start something that would create a legacy and allow me the opportunity to care of my daughter and myself. The business idea was a unique one and I knew the business would be a successful one. I worked diligently on my plan. It occupied my every free thought. I contacted suppliers and service providers, sought advice, and crunched the numbers. So, finally, after all of that planning and preparation, I decided to *do THAT thing*. I had written my vision and made it plain. All of the stars are aligned and the wheels are turning. Suddenly, the dreaded "D" word – doubt – reared its ugly head. Instead of nipping it in the bud right then, I entertained that doubt. I started second guessing myself, my abilities, and my talents. I asked myself questions like, *"Can I really do this?"* and wondered, *"Will this work?"* I fed into those thoughts and finally decided, *"Who am I fooling? I can't do this."* My business that I'd worked so hard to plan never had the opportunity to exist. My own doubt destroyed it.

For those who not only allow doubt to infiltrate their minds but also allow it to destroy their dreams, I offer two words – STOP IT! Just don't do it. Don't dwell on doubt. Your ideas and your plans can't flourish and grow when they're being choked by fear, lack of confidence, and uncertainty – all components of doubt. You have to trust yourself. As I would often say, "If you're smart enough to conjure up the idea then you're smart enough to see it through."

I purposely chose the topic of trusting yourself for the first chapter. Confidence is an essential element of achievement. Don't let doubt, second guessing, or fear cause you to miss out. That *THING* may be your chance to shine. It may be your opportunity of a lifetime, an opportunity to change your circumstances, to change someone's life, or to change the world. You never know. Why risk it all by letting doubt pull the rug from under your feet? Why let fear keep you from trusting yourself and your God-given gifts? I understand that it's not always easy to overcome self-doubt. Unfortunately, it is something everyone has dealt with it at some point in their lives. It can have a crippling effect and even leave you feeling helpless. Nevertheless, it is not impossible. It is something that can be controlled and even defeated. Years ago, I was encouraged to read a book entitled, *Feel the Fear and Do It Anyway*. In this book, the author, Dr. Susan Jeffers, reminds us that "to handle fear is to move it from a position of pain to one of power". You do this by taking that pain-producing energy (negative thoughts, negative self-talk, maintaining negative associations) and converting it into energy that gives you power (positive thinking, positive affirmations, and fruitful relationships). It was great advice and is exactly what I did. For example, I stopped saying, "I can't" (negative) even when I was unable to do something. Instead, I chose to say something like, "I can find another way to do this" (positive) or "I won't let this stop me" (positive). Therefore, yes, you can do it but only if you give up on doubt. Better yet, don't just give up on it, remove it completely. Banish it.

You may find it hard to gain the confidence you need to trust yourself, especially if you've engaged in negative self-talk or have had low self-esteem for a long time. Over time, this type of behavior does tend to develop into a habit that can be very challenging to change. I know this all too well. Growing up, I was soft-spoken and sort of timid. Words of encouragement were few and far between, and accomplishments were seldom celebrated. I loved those who were closest to me and I know they loved me but my surroundings just did not encourage self-love or personal growth. That's just the way it was. Self-love and personal growth, in my opinion, seemed frowned upon.

14

You didn't dare want to be known as a "know-it-all" or a "goody-two-shoes". Because of this, negative self-talk and feelings of inferiority took root in my life and led to years of altered self-esteem, doubt, and poor relationships. Then one day, I made a decision to longer I live an unfilled life. I needed a change and I went after it. It may have been that way for you as well. You have grown up in a household where you felt "unnoticed". You may have grown up in a single parent home where, despite all efforts, your mom or dad just couldn't make the time she or he really wanted to make for you. Whatever your reason, know that a shift from pain to power can happen for you.

I would like to say that the change I went after has already completely manifested in my life. However, in all honesty, I'm still a work in progress. You see, the kind of change that moves you from mediocre to magnificent requires healing – healing from past mistakes, poor decisions, and having your trust betrayed. It is a process. This type of healing takes patience and requires you to work at it consistently. In the end, it is a total overhaul that adjusts your attitude and renews your mind. You can do it. Throughout the next few pages, I offer a few tips to help you get there.

Tip# 1
Be Mindful of the Company You Keep

There's an adage that reminds us that, more times than not, association brings about assimilation. What does that mean? It implies that you would become more like those you are around most. That's why you should be mindful of the company you keep. Another saying – *if you want to soar with eagles, you can't flock with turkeys* – causes you to consider your associations as well. Eagles fly high. Turkeys, on the other hand, do not. Simply put – if you want to do something grand, outstanding, or even notable, you need to associate yourself with those who have done something grand, outstanding, and notable – dreamers, go-getters, high achievers.

This idiom also reminds us that it is hard to fly high when you surround yourself with those who never get themselves off of the ground. In order to evolve, you sometimes have to separate yourself. That's not to say the people you associate with are bad people. I'm not saying that at all. I'm saying you want to make sure you spend most of your time with people of aligned purpose, those going in the same direction as you or those who have already reached the destination you are striving to reach. It's important to surround yourself with those who encourage you, not discourage you or try to sway your decision to *do THAT thing.*

Beware of the dream killers. Watch out for that well-meaning person that will "encourage" you, yet secretly think you shouldn't do it or that you will fail. You know exactly who I'm talking about. There is always that one person who "knows somebody that did the same thing but it didn't work". It could be that co-worker, family member, friend, or church member that thinks your idea is a good one but will result in wasted effort. Beware of his or her negativity, usually disguised as snide remarks and limited support. I have heard many discouraging things from those who "meant well" when I shared some of my plans or business ideas with them. Perhaps you've heard statements like:

> *"That sounds like a scam to me"*

> *"You want to do what???"*

> *"Why even bother?"*

Being on the receiving end of such comments could severely hinder you trusting yourself and your abilities. I know this personally because these were just a few of the comments I heard when I shared certain dreams and ideas. While you may not be able to separate yourself completely from the "Negative Nancy" in your life, here's my advice – love them from a distance.

Earlier, I mentioned that the process of moving from mediocre to magnificent requires healing –

healing from negative thinking, healing from lack of confidence, and healing from past hurts and disappointments. A significant part of that process for me was making note of the things I wanted to change. I actually had a notebook that I kept with me almost all of the time and I would jot things down as they came to me. Once I had mustered the courage to make a solid decision to change something I had written, I would metaphorically remove it from my life by scratching or scribbling through what I'd written. It may sound silly but it was sort of life changing for me.

Take this opportunity to acknowledge a few things you may not have wanted to face before now. Sometimes it is difficult to deal with the root of an issue; however, it will give you strength and courage as you move forward in your pursuit to *do THAT thing*. Think about each of the following questions for just a moment and then write the first answers that instinctively come to mind. Address each question in the spaces provided.

Question #1

Think of those "well-meaning" individuals in your life. Who are they?

_____

_____

_____

_____

_____

_____

Action Step

Draw a line through each name if that person is nonessential to you realizing your dreams and your goals. By nonessential, I mean you do not necessarily have to share your ideas, dreams, and/or goals with this person. This person will have no significant bearing on whether or not you *do THAT thing*. By drawing the line through his or her name, you acknowledge that an effort can be made to keep this person out of your business. It is just that simple. You don't have to share any of your ideas, your goals, or your process with him or her and that's just fine.

Question #2

What are some of the snide remarks you've heard when you've shared your ideas/dreams/goals?

_____

_____

_____

_____

_____

_____

Action Step

For each snide remark listed, think of something positive to counteract them. For example, say someone said something like, "it sounds like a scam to me". Counteract by saying, "it only sounds like a scam to you because you hasn't researched the company/idea/concept". You always have the opportunity to turn what is meant to be negative into something positive.

Question #3

Express some of the emotions you experienced when you've had to deal with negativity.

_____

_____

_____

_____

_____

_____

Action Step

Dealing with the emotions caused by negative people and negative words help the process of healing. It will enable you to trust yourself. Did that snide remark make you second-guess yourself? Has a negative remark damage your ambition? Don't dwell on it. **DEAL WITH IT.** Acknowledge the emotions, replace them with increased hope and determination, and move on.

Tip #2
Watch What You Say

Earlier, I addressed converting pain-producing energy into the power you need to *do THAT thing*. One effective way to do this is by watching what you say. Sure, what others say can have an impact on how you feel and how you proceed but what you say is far more impelling. Your words are very powerful so you need to be careful about what comes out of your mouth. When I think about this lesson, I'm reminded of a defining moment for me that took place several years ago. At the time, I had been suffering from a cold or seasonal allergies (I don't quite remember which one) and my throat was really sore. I mean, it felt like I could blow flames. That's how much it hurt. I was speaking with my pastor and said to her "My throat is *killing* me." She, in turn, responded, "Watch what you say and what you're sending out into the atmosphere. Saying that your throat is killing you is giving it permission to do just that." Whoa! You talk about an eye opener! Think about it:

What you speak becomes truth for you.

So the question is – what are you sending out into the atmosphere? When it returns, will it work in your favor or will it work against you?

In your quest to reach your goals, you've probably already said something like, "I know that this is going to be hard." You've considered all of the steps you have to take, all of the systems you'll need to implement, all of the calls and all of the emails, and it may seem bit overwhelming. Professing that the process is going to be hard (before it even really gets underway) will certainly ensure that it will be. Instead, choose to say something like, "This may be a challenge but not more than I can handle." Below, I've compared two statements – one positive and the other negative. See how much they differ. Their differences will affect your dreams, your goals, and your ability to *do THAT thing* in more ways than you can probably think. Trust me. I know.

Statement #1: *"I know that this is going to be hard. I'll never be able to accomplish this."*

This statement: is negative
is painful
discourages
produces fear
makes you feel weak

Statement #2: *"This may be a bit of a challenge but it won't be more than I can handle."*

This statement: is positive
is powerful
encourages
produces hope
makes you feel strong

Lastly, develop a new speech habit by making a conscious effort to carefully choose words that support your ideas, dreams, and goals, and not hurt them. I remember when I removed the word "can't" from my vocabulary. It's such a negative word! I hated it! I felt small and weak when I said it. There is nothing small about me. I possess big dreams and a big vision. And there is certainly nothing weak about me. I can roll with the best of them. So why was I allowing this little four-letter word make me feel like that? From there, I made a decision to get rid of it. Was it easy? Actually, it was. All I had to do was think before I spoke. Instead of saying, "I can't make it", say "I'll have to join you another time." See? I told you! Easy peasy!

Tip #3
Use Positive Affirmations

You can begin developing a new speech habit by using positive affirmations. Consistently use statements that help you overcome negative thoughts. It could be just one sentence or a phrase. Speak to yourself. Tell yourself how smart you are to have such a great idea. Speak about all of the support you anticipate while pursuing your endeavors. It may be a little weird at first but, trust me, it is very effective. Some would say it's even therapeutic. There is a powerful quote from Philip K. Dick's *VALIS* that says, "There exists, for everyone, a sentence - a series of words - that has the power to destroy you. Another sentence exists, another series of words, that could heal you". This quote certainly adds depth to the take on the power of words. The first series of words are negative, words that cut & destroy. The second series of words – refreshing. Use words to your advantage with positive affirmations.

When I was first introduced to affirmations, I must admit, it seemed a little foreign to me. Honestly, it even seemed ridiculous. Before you judge me, hear me out. I was one of those that had to see it to believe it. Yep. I was *that* person. Faith, at first, just didn't come naturally for me. I really struggled in that area. So I studied the concepts behind faith and using words to create your world. I read accounts of people whose lives were completely changed because they chose to be positive and speak positively. I listened to testimonies of friends and family members on how proclaiming what they wanted, through words, worked in their favor. I figured so many people couldn't be wrong. I decided to do it. I started with, "I am fearfully and wonderfully made" (Psalms 139:14 MSG). Over the years, it has changed a bit. More recently, I read this affirmation somewhere. They're not my words but adopted them, and, today, I speak it into my life daily. It reads:

The me TODAY is STRONG

The me TODAY is DETERMINED

The me TODAY is ABUNDANT

The me TODAY is WORTHY

The me TODAY is ABLE

The me TODAY is PASSIONATE

The me TODAY is WILLING

The me TODAY is WORKING

The me TODAY is MOVING MOUNTAINS

The me TODAY can do ANYTHING.

Now it's your turn! Use the space provided to write yours. Don't have one? Create one. Think about your goals/career/business and how you'd like to see it evolve and grow. Write those thoughts. As you write it, speak it. Let it speak to you. Let it encourage you. Ready…set…GO!

What do YOU affirm? Write it here.

_____

_____

_____

_____

_____

_____

_____

_____

_____

_____

_____

_____

_____

_____

_____

_____

Tip #4
See Yourself There

This tip goes hand in hand with the previous tip – speaking positive affirmations. Speak it then see it. Envision your success. Think about all of those reasons you want to *do THAT thing*. Imagine yourself helping someone. Consider what pursuing your dream, your goal, or your vision could mean for your future or your family's future. Seeing yourself there can be the final step needed to propel you forward. I used this practice myself to get my business off the ground. I envisioned a successful business. I saw myself speaking on the subject of entrepreneurship. I saw myself coaching new business owners. What once was an idea has become my reality and envisioning my success is where it started. Seeing yourself there must be accompanied by action, of course. You will need to design a course of action best suited to helping you meet your goal.

When you have reached that point, where you can replace doubt with trust, you have confidently decided that someone somewhere needs what you have to offer. You know, without a shadow of a doubt, that once you *do THAT thing*, what you produce will be cultivated into something wonderful. Just picture it – a confident you, ready and equipped to conquer fear, doubt, and anything else that comes your way. When I began writing this very book you hold in your hands, I saw myself as a published author first. I saw myself there, even before I started. I knew how passionate I was about completing a project that I knew was divinely in line with my purpose. I saw myself working long hours, sometimes through the night, to produce my best. I saw myself telling the world about it and why I wrote it. I saw success. I saw myself there. Now, you may be thinking that this practice is…well, preposterous. You may even be thinking that your goals and dreams are too far-fetched, for whatever reason. I challenge you to reconsider. Give yourself a chance. Think about all of the great discoveries, ideas, and inventions that surround you on a daily basis. Most of them, if not all, started in the minds of individuals who envisioned the end product before they could even find the right words to explain what it was. They probably endured ridicule; skepticism from family and friends; taunts from naysayers. Nevertheless, they did not let it stop them. If they had, we probably would not be able to enjoy many of the modern conveniences or luxuries (like television, automobiles, and the list goes on) that we do today. These individuals passionately pursued their visions and knew someone somewhere needed that they had to offer. They put their shoulders to the wheel and gave it their all because they saw themselves there first.

2

Be Original – But Don't Reinvent the Wheel

Don't try and reinvent the wheel –
just work on making it better than anyone else.

John Muir

When you consider making the very important decision to *do THAT thing*, remember that you don't have to "reinvent the wheel." You don't necessarily have to come up with a completely new idea. You can simply make an existing idea, product, career, and/or business your own. Unless you're producing a brand new product or introducing some new invention or technology, more than likely someone has already had the same idea. A wise man once said that "there is nothing new under the sun." There are many products that were created from "recycled ideas". One look at fashion trends would prove that there truly is nothing new. For instance, platform shoes were a huge fashion trend in the 1970s. Forty years later, we're wearing them again. There are many new styles and new designers but the original concept remains. As you prepare to *do THAT thing*, chances are you aren't the first one to come up with that great idea you have. While that may sound a little disheartening, don't let it stop you. Just think. There are loads of great products and services available in this day and age that are totally different from what they were five, ten, twenty years ago. Some change from year to year. For example, look at the evolution of the smartphone. One of the first created, the Simon Personal Communicator, was introduced in the early 1990s by IBM. It had some of the same features that we enjoy with today's smartphones – touchscreen, apps, and games – but it weighed over a pound and cost almost $900! Primitive in its design, changes were imminent if the concept of the smartphone was to survive. Fast forward twenty years later and phone manufacturers have developed products with the same basic technology but totally different. These companies didn't reinvent the wheel. They simply improved upon an idea that already existed and made it their own.

Making an idea your own starts with you.

You have to lay that claim and hold onto it. When I started my first business – GIME LLC – in 2009, I was excited about becoming a business owner. My business allowed me the opportunity to work from the comforts of my home, provided the flexibility I needed as a single mother with school-aged children, and the ability to determine my own paycheck. It was exciting! So exciting, I didn't want to keep it to myself. The following year began the start of my second business venture, designed to encourage and help women explore the "wonderful world of entrepreneurship" and all of its benefits. I wanted women to know that they could own and run successful businesses. So I began my research and found that there were literally thousands of companies already doing this, many of which were already very successful brands. Whoa! You talk about a wrench in my spokes! It's not like I didn't know these companies existed. It was because of one such company that I started my business. Nevertheless, I was overcome with feelings of incompetency. *Women won't be interested in what I have to say when they can just go to one of these bigger brands,* I thought. I was so discouraged that I decided to just work my business and be happy with that. If someone asked for my help in starting a business or needed some business advice, I would graciously lend my expertise. However, the goal of making it my business to reach out to women was placed on the back burner. A year later, I explored the idea again. This time, I was armed with and enlightened on the principles of finding a *niche* – a specialized, or targeted, market.

> ***Very narrow areas of expertise can be very productive.***
> ***Develop your profile. Develop your niche.***
> **Leigh Steinberg**

Finding a niche is how you make an idea your own. It personalizes what **YOU** do, how **YOU** do it, and who **YOU** share it with. As you develop your niche, you become somewhat of a subject matter expert. Pretty cool, huh? Here's how the concept works. Let's say you love to travel and have done a good bit of traveling abroad. Because of your extensive knowledge of traveling abroad, you decided to *do THAT thing* and start a blog about traveling. Well, there are already many other bloggers out there who talk about traveling. How do you make it your own? Consider the countries you've visited. With which country do you feel you have enough knowledge to consider yourself a comprehensive source to anyone traveling to the area? Let's say, for example, you've lived in France during summer breaks while in college and you've visited every other year since. You know how to interact with French natives, are fluent in the language, and have the inside scoop on unique places to see and things to do beyond the regular "touristy" things. Great! You have entered "niche territory". You aren't reinventing the wheel here. You're simply being original in your own rite. Now, you have shifted from being a travel blogger to being a blogger who shares personal experiences from travel through France. Your niche can be narrowed down even further, based on your experiences as: a woman traveling alone, or as a retired individual, or as a family with children, or whatever. This is how finding a niche works. It's sort of like reducing fractions (for all of you who remember that stuff from elementary school). You take a broad range of experiences and break them down to the smallest common denominator.

Let me see if you actually get the idea of finding a niche. Consider the following scenario. Take its broad range and reduce it down to a specialty, or niche:

> You are a recent college graduate with a degree in special education and have gained employment with one of the top schools in your area dedicated to the education of children with special needs. You knew, since you were in middle school, that special education was a field of interest you would pursue especially after

learning that your younger sister was diagnosed as autistic. Throughout high school, you were very close with your sister and, despite her diagnosis, you recognized advances in her behavior and social interaction through a certain game the two of you would often play. It was a simple game that you made up but every time you'd play it with her, she would shows changes in her participation, like she would remember the rules or would be more expressive. While in college, you volunteered at a local facility for children with special needs. Your game followed you and, as you played with the children there, you realized that your "simple game" had the same effect on these children as well. It was then that you recognized your genius. There are at least two niche areas that can be complied from this scenario. What do you think? Write it in the space provided.

_____

_____

_____

_____

_____

_____

Now that I have your wheels turning, let's do something fun. There's no scenario this time. We're going to talk about YOU. Many times, we don't realize how awesome we are. We overlook our own greatness. I want you to point out your own gifts and talents. Use the space below to jot down a few of the things you're really good at. For example, if you bake a mean sweet potato pie or if your crocheted gifts have been wrapped around or worn on the heads of more babies than you can remember, add those gifts and talents to the list.

I ROCK when it comes to:

_____

_____

_____

_____

From your list, circle your top three choices. Of those top three choices, choose one that you really have a passion for and highlight it. If you're thinking, "I am my happiest every opportunity I get to *do THAT thing,* but I wouldn't say it's a passion", consider this. If it's not your main source of income but you'll do it every chance you get, then it is a passion. If you could *do THAT thing* every day and would be satisfied, then it is a passion. It may even be that side hustle (because *everyone* has a side hustle). What is that passion?

I recognize my passion!

_____

_____

_____

Many have turned their passion into profitable businesses. You've probably read stories about people who have turned their passion into a paycheck or even know someone personally who has. I've watched my cousin turn her passion for braiding hair into a paycheck. I've seen a friend turn his passion for music into a paycheck as a popular DJ. Even I have experienced turning my passion for working with entrepreneurs and small business owners into a paycheck. If that's your desire, you can too.

Being original, in your own right, does not only apply to starting a business. There are no restrictions here. Take a look at any aspect of your life. That's what I did when I originally grasped this concept. I took a hard look at my life and realized I was putting too much energy into trying to be like someone others wanted or expected me to be. For years, I'd heard things like, "You should be..." and "I think you should...". So I starting thinking, "Well, maybe I should be..." and worked hard to be who someone else wanted me to be. I'm not discounting the potential others saw in me or the faith others had in my abilities but trying to live up to everyone else's expectations was exhausting! So guess what I did? Instead of being like everyone else, I chose to be original in my own right. I personally chose to release that free-spirited person that had been tucked away in my innermost being. I'd always felt so different from everyone else around me – not better than but just different from. As a child, I dreamed a lot and envisioned myself being and living unlike anyone I knew personally. I remember promising myself that, one day, I was going to break away from the "cookie cutter" mentality because I felt I was destined to be different. Gradually, I began my shift and, you know what? It wasn't so bad. It didn't hurt and it certainly didn't take me out. So I shifted a little bit more, becoming more open minded and more of an outside the box thinker and doer. I tried new things and I went new places. I connected with new people (but not too many, thanks to my introversion issues...lol) and I even changed my hair! I'm now a happier person all because I chose to *do THAT thing*, and for me that meant stepping outside the box! So what's **THAT** thing for you? This is what I mean when I say originality can be applied to any aspect of your life, even when it comes to choosing to express yourself differently.

Yay...yay...yay! It's time to get those creative juices flowing again! I am certain that there are a few things you can add your personal touch or flair to that would turn the ordinary into the extraordinary. Right now, I want you to think on just two of them. It could be anything. For example, being original without reinventing the wheel can be applied to how you celebrate holidays. You can make an event or celebration your own by incorporating fresh, new ideas versus those set by traditions. I know someone who, instead of celebrating Christmas in its traditional sense, chooses to celebrate by taking an exotic vacation during that time of year. I think it is a pretty cool idea and may even implement that one into my own life. *An annual exotic vacation...hmmmm.* Whoa! I had to reel myself back in from that thought! But really, let's focus on you. I want you to realize that which is on the inside of you. You may not recognize the creativity or perhaps have just kept hidden. It's time to unleash it. Use the following spaces to discuss those two things that you can take from *ordinary* to EXTRAORDINARY.

Move from *ordinary*...

_____

_____

_____

_____

_____

_____

to *EXTRAORDINARY!!*

_____

_____

_____

_____

_____

Move from *ordinary…*

_____

_____

_____

_____

_____

_____

to *EXTRAORDINARY!!*

_____

_____

_____

_____

_____

3

Don't Go It Alone

If you want to go fast, go alone.
If you want to go far, go together.
African proverb

No man is an island. Everybody needs somebody. In order to *do THAT thing*, you should not expect to do it alone. Why would you want to? I understand that you may be sort of a loner (so am I) and you may be a bit of an introvert (I am too) but, in actuality, you do need others. You need a circle of supporters. Your circle does not have to be a huge one. For instance, my circle is so small, I'm barely in it! LOL!!! But all jokes aside, you do need the support of –

(1) those who you love and who genuinely love you, and
(2) those that have proven to be trustworthy

Consider the aforementioned African proverb and think about it for a moment. If you've gone somewhere, maybe on a road trip, by yourself, doesn't it often time seem like the trip takes forever? Now think about that same road trip, but this time, consider having your friends along with you. It doesn't even matter how far you have to travel, as long as you all are together, you seem to get there before you even know it.

Having a circle of supporters, encouragers, and even a mentor will work to help you in reaching your goals. Before you even know it, you'll be there. Just know that those who've crossed your path have done so for a reason. You may not realize it at the time but everyone in your circle has a purpose. Consider the co-worker you met years ago. You connected with her, at the time, because you worked closely with her every day. However, it's been years since you two have gone your separate ways yet the two of you have kept in touch. Today, she organizes and hosts events centered on issues she's passionate about – fitness and nutrition. You think, "How awesome and courageous she is to step out and do something she has always wanted to do." You, too, have always wanted to host events that exhibit your passion but just didn't know how to go about doing so. Now you have someone who (1) started with an idea, (2) figured out how to turn that idea into a successful event, and (3) took the steps to bring it into fruition. She is now someone that you know personally who has "been there and done that" that you can turn to for guidance and advice. The woman you met years ago who sat across from you and with whom you shared lunch, laughs and conversation has become a mentor. Who knew?

48

This is why it is important to foster genuine relationships. Note that I said genuine relationships. There is no doubt that you will meet many different people for many different reasons throughout your lifetime. Some people will be in your life only for that season of your life. By saying "season", I'm simply referring to that period in your life. It could be during high school or college. A season could be your time serving in the military or during a particular period of employment. Whatever the season is, if that person is "seasonal", he or she will become sort of an afterthought once the season is over. For example, you probably had lots of "friends" during college. Aren't there a few whose names you can't even remember? When you talk about him or her, you say something like, "I can't think of her name but she always wore a hat and drove a little blue car." I know you're laughing because it's true. That person was seasonal and now that that season of your life is over, she has become just a thought. It happens all of the time. Then, there are those you meet who become intentional in your life. I call these your genuine relationships. These are the ones where, when you meet, you connect on a level that is meaningful. You share something that creates a bond that last beyond a season.

Genuine relationships stick around for the long haul.

Consider a few of your genuine relationships. Although you may not see each other often, when you do, you pick up right where you left off, right? When you're together, there's a good time to be had by all, right? Yes? That's a genuine relationship – a connection with a trusted individual that understands you, recognizes the good (and the not-so-good) in you, and is there for you, despite distance, time or space. In your circle, these individuals are your supporters and encouragers. You should have at least three people in your life with whom you can:

(1) **tell** *ANYTHING* **to** – from the good news to those deep things that you may not want anyone to know but you have to tell someone or else you'll lose your mind;

(2) **cry in front of** – and, yes, I mean an ugly cry where the mascara is running, the nose is running and you can barely get the words out between sniffles;

(3) **expect an honest opinion from** – you don't need anyone trying to sugar-coat anything for you, especially when you want to *do THAT thing*;

(4) **depend on** – for the small things and the big things; everyone needs someone they can call on when they're in a jam or when they need help;

(5) **laugh with** – laughter is an important element that helps to lighten the mood when things are challenging or difficult.

For me, one of my relationships, with an individual whom I've known for over twenty years, almost always serves up good times and lots of laughter. We don't necessarily talk to each other on a regular basis, but, when we do, we share and we laugh. On the flip side, we have also been able to shed tears together. I also have friends that I can discuss my goals, my ideas, and my challenges with and expect them to provide advice or an opinion that is impartial.

Share a little bit about your three relationships in the following spaces. Who are these three individuals? Think back to when and how you met him or her. How has your relationship grown or changed over the years? Why do you consider him or her a genuine friend? Consider all of that as you fill in the spaces on the next few pages.

A little bit about _____

_____

_____

_____

_____

_____

_____

_____

_____

_____

_____

_____

_____

_____

_____

_____

_____

_____

A little bit about _____

_____

_____

_____

_____

_____

_____

_____

_____

_____

_____

_____

_____

_____

_____

_____

_____

_____

_____

_____

A little bit about _____

_____

_____

_____

_____

_____

_____

_____

_____

_____

_____

_____

_____

_____

_____

_____

_____

_____

_____

So we know it is important to have the support and encouragement of good friends and family as you take your leap of faith. It is also important to connect with others who are doing what you want to do, or something pretty similar, and don't mind sharing their experiences with you or showing you how you can do it too. These individuals we call coaches. According to Merriam-Webster, a coach is "one who instructs or trains". Even the most talented professionals in the world have coaches. Consider professional athletes, for example. While these athletes possess the talent, skills, and abilities, the coach is there to encourage each player's potential and motivate their greatness. A coach strategically manages the athlete's performance. Throughout the game, the coach is always watching and guiding, changing a play as necessary. This is why you need a coach as you *do THAT thing*. So if you were thinking that coaches are restricted to athletes, think again. Dancers have coaches. Students have coaches. Even coaches employ coaches, especially when seeking advancement and expansion, and you should too.

Here's what I thought of the first time I considered working with a coach – that if I shared my goals and ideas with this person, those ideas would be "stolen". Silly, huh? I blame my apprehension on some stories I heard of someone that trusted someone else with their ideas and then that someone else ran off with them. Those stories alone can cause anyone to be a little overly cautious. That's why it's important to do your research and make sure that the person you choose to trust with your dreams is indeed trustworthy. When I finally decided on my coach, it had been after two years of research. I followed her on her social media outlets. I listened to via her chats and/or podcasts, just watching and evaluating her. In those two years, I found that we were alike in a number of ways. I had decided that she was someone who was doing what I wanted to do and on the level in which I wanted to get to. She was open, honest, and most of all, fearless! She was definitely someone I wanted to learn from. With that said, you would certainly want to consider the following five tips, at minimum, when choosing a coach:

1. **Go for the expert** – This is your dream we're talking about. Go all out! Seek someone who knows his or her stuff and is a known expert in his or her field. An expert is sure to give you the latest advice. Why? Because an expert in his or her field is continuously learning and takes pride in learning new skills.

2. **Choose someone with experience as a coach and personal experience in your area of interest as well** – This one...kind of a no-brainer. How can you expect someone to coach you in an area in which he or she has no actual experience?

3. **Get testimonials** – Talk with the people your prospective coach has served. You can learn a lot from these individuals, as they were once where you are – trying to make a decision as to whether or not they would work with the coach. Ask every question you can think of. Were they coached an area of interest similar to yours? How consistent was the coach? Ask questions regarding the coach's punctuality, commitment to schedule, follow-up procedures, etc.

4. **Check your prospective coach's knowledge level** – Coaching is a skill and it takes practice and experience to master them. Does your prospective coach have what it takes? I mean, you will be picking his or her brain to learn from what it you're seeking to learn.

5. **Make sure who you choose is a good fit for you** – Yes, it's great to find a person who give expert advice because he or she has a gazillion years of experience and all of the testimonials to back it up. All of that is great but how do you feel about the person as a person. Are you comfortable with him or her? Is the person a good fit personality-wise? You wouldn't want someone that quiet and reserved if you're an outgoing and energetic individual, right? Consider the way you feel after speaking with him or her. Do you feel positive and uplifted? You should but if you don't, that coach may not be the one for you.

In addition to having great friends and/or family members you can depend on and working with a great coach, I encourage you to connect with others through networking. There's just something about being around those who are like-minded and forward-moving. It's encouraging. It's motivating. I've been connected to a number of networking groups over the years. I often attend networking events to meet new people and learn new things. As you set out to *do THAT thing*, you'll find that your journey will connect you with many people. Some of those you connect with will be from a background similar to yours while others will hail from a background that's totally different. You'll meet people in careers and fields of expertise that you've never heard of. This is the beauty of networking. Embrace it. I've actually met some pretty interesting people simply through networking. Once, I met someone who has established and currently runs a private school. We actually became friends, especially after finding out we share the same birthday! Another time, I had the pleasure of meeting someone who turns balloons into masterpieces. Over the years, I've even met individuals who have left professional careers as engineers, lawyers, and corporate executives to *do THAT thing* they've always wanted to do. They found the courage to trust themselves, sought expert advice, and connected with others who were doing what they wanted to do. Because of this, they were confident that they could *do THAT thing* and guess what? THEY DID IT!

It's all about making those connections and then nurturing them. How do you nurture your relationships? You send thank you notes or other expressions of gratitude. You support their events and ask how you can help their efforts. You create a *win-win situation* – a relationship in which you give something (your time, your talent, your expertise, your financial support, etc.) and you get something of equal or greater value in return. From time to time, as you *do THAT thing*, you may need to pick someone's brain. You may need someone to make a call on your behalf that will open a door of opportunity for you. A nurtured connection could do this for you.

4

Believe In You

*You have to believe in yourself when no one else does –
that makes you a winner right there.*

Venus Williams

I have always considered myself a smart girl – always thinking, always envisioning, and always creating. Despite that which had always been in me, there were many times when I simply didn't believe in myself. Sometimes, I would think things like, *"This vision of success can't be for me."* or something like, *"I have all of these plans but there's no way they were all meant for me."* Growing up, I stifled my creativity so much, it became second nature. You see, I came from very humble beginnings and creativity wasn't high on the list of priorities. Raised in a small rural town where everyone knew everyone, there wasn't much exposure to anything more than what went on in our small community. Nevertheless, I would dream of doing big things one day. I remember having a composition notebook that I called my "dream book". In it, I wrote plans for my future. It included pictures of things I wanted and places I wanted to go. I had no idea how it was going to happen, but I was certain that they would become my reality. So I waited. I waited on my family to tell me that they believed in me and that I can do whatever I set out to do. I waited on my friends to pat me on the back and cheer me on. I waited for someone influential to grab me by the hand and mentor me to success. Guess what? It didn't quite turn out that way. I was on my own in pursuing my dreams.

Your story may be similar to mine. You may have felt this way – desperate and overwhelmed – at some point in your life. You've looked to others, expecting those closest to you to believe in your dream enough to stop everything they're doing and nurture your process. Unfortunately, it almost never happens that way. The job of believing in you belongs to you. I'll say that again –

The job of believing in YOU belongs to YOU.

When no one else can see the method to your madness, you believe in you. When no one else trusts your ideas, you believe in you. The same is true for the opposite. Even when everyone else can see the method to your madness and even trust your ideas, YOU still have to believe in YOU. Yes, you do. You have to always be your biggest cheerleader and your own biggest supporter.

Believing in you doesn't always come easy. Some of us are just so hard on ourselves! We work so hard to be perfect, knowing good and well that perfection is unattainable. Nevertheless, when perfection doesn't happen, we tend to stop believing. DON'T DO THAT! Seeing your ideas become reality is not so far-fetched. Simply have plan and then make it work. And don't be so quick to throw in the towel. Chances are things may not work on your first attempt. If it doesn't, know you're in good company:

- Abraham Lincoln ran for several public office appointments (state legislature, Congress, Senate) and was often defeated before becoming the President of the United States. He didn't give up. I imagine he believed in himself.

- Michael Jordan, who many consider the greatest basketball player of all time, was cut from his high school basketball team. I imagine he realized the greatness within him. He kept at it and didn't let one failure stop him. I imagine he believed in himself.

- J. K. Rolling, author of the Harry Potter book series, was broke and depressed when she started. I can relate, having been in a very similar situation – divorced and struggling to raise my children. She turned her lemons into lemonade. I imagine she believed in herself.

- Oprah Winfrey – one of the richest and most successful women in the world – was once said to be "unfit for television". (I bet whoever said that and fired her is thinking twice now). She didn't give up and we all know how the story goes. I imagine she believed in herself.

These are just a few examples of individuals who believed in themselves. Yeah, they're famous and their stories have been made public but, trust me, there are many everyday people who have similar stories. I am a prime example. I made several attempts, over the years, at unleashing my greatness and failed miserably. Failure didn't stop me because I knew that if one approach doesn't work, it is alright to try another approach. There is a quote by Claire Cook, author of *Seven Year Switch*, which says, "If plan A doesn't work, the alphabet has 25 more letters – 204 if you're in Japan."

Believing in you means you give yourself as many opportunities as needed to be great. Always be willing to try again. Consider greatness as your destiny and don't let anything stop you until you reach it. In the process, you will be tested. It is inevitable. Think about what we've already discussed in the previous chapters. First, doubt and fear tried to hinder your moves. They put up as a good fight in their efforts to keep you bound. Just as you get a handle on those emotions, you tackled the need to deal with the people closest to you who attempt to sway you away from your decision to *do THAT thing*. You come out the victor in yet another fight and have managed to separate yourself from the naysayers. You're on a roll but now you come up against your biggest enemy – YOU. You've already conquered so much at this point. Are you going to stop here because you refuse to believe you can *do THAT thing*? It is said that "the temptation to quit will be greatest just before you are about to succeed". Please…please…please! Don't give up!

Perseverance is a main ingredient in believing in you. By definition, the word itself describes "steadfastness, despite difficulty, in achieving success." Let's break that definition down:

1. **steadfastness** – In your quest to *do THAT thing*, you may be moved (by various situations and/or circumstances) but you don't change. You remain very loyal to how you feel and what you believe in.

2. **despite** – Things will happen. According to Murphy's Law, "anything that can go wrong will go wrong". With that in mind, keep going in spite of the hiccups along the way. You develop tough skin and become unstoppable.

3. **difficulty** – Working on fulfilling your dreams can be challenging no matter who you are. Ecclesiastes 9:11 (NIV) reminds us that, "the race is not to the swift, or the battle to the strong, nor does food come to the brilliant or favor to the learned; but time and chance happen to them all." In other words, difficulty befalls us all. You will sometimes be disappointed. You will feel overwhelmed. You will hear "no" more times than you would like. You persevere, no matter what, if you want to *do THAT thing*.

Perseverance means you believe in your goals and your dream to such an extent that you don't give up. You just keep at it – consistently. You are intentional in the things you do that get you one step closer to meeting your goals. In order to *do THAT thing*, you work it! You push, you press, but you don't stop. Perseverance, however, doesn't always come easily. It is a trait that must be cultivated on a daily basis. In the beginning, I struggled in this area. Being the free spirit that I am, I'd been used to taking things as they come. I had no real plan for my success. (Do you remember when I talked about myself, always doing "stuff"?) However, when I decided I wanted to build a successful business and brand, things had to change. I did know a thing or two about getting what I wanted so I took that knowledge and applied it to my business. I had to make calls that took me out of my comfort zone. I had to approach people who were sort of intimidating. Nevertheless, I did it because I believed in my vision. How much do you believe in your vision? Enough to give it your all? Yes? YES!!!

When you believe in yourself, there is no stopping you. When someone tells "no", you don't let it stop you. When a door is closed on an opportunity, you try another door. Everything you do in pursuit of THAT thing is intentional. That means every call you make, every word you write, every person you talk to, and everything you do is on purpose. You leave nothing to chance because your dreams and your goals are just too important.

> *And you never climb a mountain on accident*
> *— it has to be intentional.*
> **Mark Udall**

Use this quote has an example. Once you've decided to climb a mountain, do you just go for it? I don't think you would. I know wouldn't, especially since I've never climbed a mountain before. First, I would prepare by training, making sure I'm fit enough to endure the climb. Then, I would also make sure I have all of the necessary gear. All the while, I'd prepare mentally by believing that I can and I will climb that mountain. Don't get me wrong.

I'm a fan of spontaneity but not when deciding to climb a mountain, and certainly not when I'd decided to *do THAT thing.*

When you believe in you, you make sure the way is made as clearly as possible, increasing your chances of success. Look back at the mountain climbing example. You would not want to approach that feat, especially for the first time, when unpredictable weather is forecasted. Doing so could possibly diminish your possibilities of a successful climb. Think about your goals and your dreams in that manner as well. Always consider what you can do to increase your chances of successfully reaching them. Here are just a few ways you can do that –

1. **Abandon your expectations.** Why not approach a new and unfamiliar situation with an open mind? While you may know someone who has done something you want to do, do not allow their experience to create your expectation. Your outcome could be totally different. For example, your friend has had a particularly challenging experience in direct sales, and you've been considering entering that field. Will you allow your friend's experience to stop you from entering the field or will you join the field with the expectation of overwhelming challenges? I would not advise you to do either. Go in with an open mind. Open yourself up to the possibility of success. You just never know how it will pan out for you.

2. **Let go of the past.** You made a mistake in the past but you are still holding onto it. Why? Do you feel that no one will see past the mistake? Does the mistake cater to

your fears and give an excuse when you want to cop out? Stop using that mistake as a wall that keeps you in bondage. Instead, use it as a stepping stone to get you moving in the right direction. I cannot begin to tell you all of the mistakes I've made – from trusting the wrong people to mismanaging my time to being wasteful irresponsible with my finances. I did not, however, let my mistakes stop me moving forward. I mean, everyone makes mistakes. Don't beat yourself up about it. What I would encourage you to do is (1) recognize where you went wrong, (2) make a conscious effort to avoid the individual, situation, or circumstance responsible for contributing to that mistake, and (3) let it go.

3. **Take time to celebrate your accomplishments.** This should be an automatic but guess what? It isn't. You work hard. You get a lot done. You experience long days and even longer nights. And when it is all said and done, yes, you come out on top. Then, it is on to the next goal. Before to jump to the next thing, wait a minute. Stop! Breathe! Take time to celebrate your success. I recently grasped this concept and now, when I set a personal or business goal, I also establish a reward for my successful completion. It does not have to be anything extravagant. For example, I had a goal for helping at least three entrepreneurs start their businesses within thirty days. When I accomplished that goal, I rewarded myself with lunch at one of my favorite restaurants. You can set whatever reward you want. I have heard others celebrate their accomplishments by going to see a show or movie, buying a new dress or pair of shoes, or even treating themselves to a weekend getaway. It really does not

matter what you decide on as your reward. If you feel you deserve it as a result of all of your hard work, then just do it. Do not let anyone else dictate how you should reward yourself and your accomplishments. Make it fun and you make it about you.

5

Make the Decision and Go for It

It always seems impossible until it's done.
Nelson Mandela

Yes! Yes! Yes! You've made the decision to *do THAT thing*. You're ready to #gobegreat! You are excited and I am excited for you! You are finally giving your gifts and talents the chance to flourish and it is time for the rubber to hit the road! Be sure, as you set out on this amazingly courageous journey, that you are equipped with your roadmap. You would never travel without an itinerary, right? Picture this – you're taking an international trip. You prepare by making sure you have a passport, proper immunizations, etc. Before the flight, you familiarize yourself with airport etiquette. Once at the airport, you compile all the information regarding your flight – your flight number, your departing gate, and the boarding time. Am I right? Consider the same for a road trip. In this instance, you choose a route & decide which roads to take to get you from point A to point B. If you anticipate weather concerns, you may even map out ways to navigate around expected roadblocks and detours. To *do THAT thing*, you need an itinerary as well. My experience has taught me that there are a few essentials you'll need when pursuing any endeavor. From those experiences, I have created what I call *The D.R.E.A.M Roadmap* and I gladly share it with you.

The D.R.E.A.M Roadmap focuses on five elements – (1) Due Diligence; (2) Resources; (3) Effective Systems; (4) Accountability Partnerships; and (5) Management of Your Time. These elements are designed to work together to ensure that you *do THAT thing* and do it well. The next few pages will explore the importance of each essential of *The D.R.E.A.M Roadmap*.

D.R.E.A.M Essential #1
Due Diligence

Before you do anything, you should always want to do your own research. It's alright if what someone shared with you sparked your interest. He or she can make an idea or business opportunity sounds so amazing, like it was meant for you. Despite how convincing the person may be or despite how much you may trust the individual, it pays to look into whatever it is for yourself. This is what we called due diligence.

Due diligence is defined as "the care that a reasonable person exercises to avoid harm to other persons or their property." Another definition goes on to define it as "research and analysis of a company or organization done in preparation for a business transaction." I want you to read those definitions again. Go ahead. I'll wait. From the two definitions, pull out the following keywords – **care**, **reasonable**, **avoid**, **research and analysis** and **preparation**. These are some pretty important words, especially in regards to your decision to "do THAT thing". Let's take an in-depth look into each word.

> 1. *Care* – Your idea/dream/goal is like a baby. It requires lots of love and attention. Without love and attention, a baby won't develop to its full potential. A baby needs proper nourishment. Without it, a baby won't grow. It won't thrive. It will die. Take care in giving your idea/dream/goal everything it needs – your time, attention & dedication. Trust me. It will blossom into the greatness you always hoped it would.

> 2. *Reasonable* – To be reasonable is to be sensible. In other words, a reasonable person uses common sense. Do you remember, when you

were younger, how you would do something that was just so irresponsible and ridiculous, your parents would ask something like, "You certainly didn't use any common sense!" In other words, they recognized that, despite everything they've taught you about what's right and what's wrong, you chose poor judgment over sound judgment. You have to use sound judgment as you set out to *do THAT thing*. Being reasonable will cause you to be aware and think before you act. I'm not saying not to take risks. Sometimes, you'll have to. But be wise in your risk taking. I'm sure you've heard the saying, "If it sounds too good to be true, it probably is." Think about that each time you consider a decision regarding your goals.

3. Avoid Harm – Remember when I referred to your idea/dream/goal as your "baby"? Would you allow someone or something to hurt your "baby"? Will you allow your "baby" to be taken or snatched away from you without a fight? I bet you won't. I know I wouldn't. Your "baby" is precious and needs your protection. That's why due diligence is so important. Always dot your I's and cross your T's. Ensure the successful development of your "baby" by avoiding pitfalls and other dangerous situations. How do you do that? Here are a few suggestions:

- Make sure your dealings are legit and those who you associate with operate legitimately

- Check credentials, accreditations, licenses, etc. by research public records
- Always ask from references

4. *Research and Analysis* – This is a very important step in performing your due diligence. This is where you become sort of a detective in pursuit of your own success. Yep! This is where you can poke, pry, and be as nosy as you'd like. It's my favorite part of the process. Personally, I begin with a simple inquiry using my favorite search engine. When I started GIME LLC in 2009, I went to Google and typed "work from home opportunity". There were over a million of results. "Boy, oh boy!" I thought. It was obvious that I needed to be more specific so the search results would be narrowed down. Then I typed something like "legitimate work from home opportunity better business bureau credentials". I know it sounds a little ridiculous, but sometimes that's what it takes. When I saw a few of the same business names coming up in every search, I began analyzing each company individually. I compared their strengths and weaknesses, their startup fees, and what others had to say about them. Was that too much? Nope. It's never too much if you want to "do THAT thing" and do it right.

5. *Preparation* – Be prepared for the expected and for the unexpected. There will be some things you just cannot prepare for and there will be

events that are out of your control. However, when you CAN be prepared, do so. I have to admit. Being prepared has not always been one of my strengths. This was a skill I had to work on. Either I had one part ready and was still working on the other part or I had more work to do because something occurred that I didn't anticipate. Then, one day, a light bulb came on. I heard someone say what I considered to be so profound –

Don't have to *get* ready; *stay* ready.

From that point on, I was committed to staying ready by always being prepared. Here are few things I've learned along the way that can help anyone to be prepared and stay ready:

- **Start from the inside out.** You may not always be able to control the things that go on around you but you definitely have a say in how you react to them. Develop your survival skills and prepare yourself mentally so you can be ready for anything that comes your way.

- **Know exactly what you want.** You can't straddle the fence here. You have to know precisely what your goals are in order to be prepared in your pursuit to greatness.

- **Know what you will accept and what you will not accept.** Being prepared in this way will allow you to avoid be persuaded or pressured to make a decision you know won't be a good fit for you.

D.R.E.A.M Essential #2
Resources

Most of the time, when someone says "resources", we automatically think money. Yes, having money or access to money is important because "it takes money to make money" (I'm certain you've heard that before). However, there are other types of resources that you'll need access to. My top two are:

1. **People** – Most corporate entities have established that their people are their most important resource. Nothing runs without people to run it. While many of today's processes are automated and computerized, people still top the charts when it comes to the resources needed to run a successful operation. When you do THAT thing, you need people in your corner – people who have experience, people that can offer advice and suggestions. You'll need people to encourage you & to be a helping hand. You'll need people to brainstorm with, to listen to your ideas, and to give you their opinions. You may even need some people to work their "magic" on your behalf, creating an opportunity for you that you couldn't orchestrate by yourself. Some of the people in my life when I started my entrepreneurial journey were instrumental in my business success. I probably wouldn't have even started my business, Better Business Solutions, if it weren't for someone listening to my ideas and encouraging me. And once I actually got the business up and running, that same someone worked a little "magic" on my business' behalf. I'm sure you've heard it said that, "it's not always *what* you know but *who* you know". As you do THAT thing, you might find this to be more than not.

2. **Plan** – There's nothing like a well laid out plan. Ask me how I know. This is something I learned after an opportunity was presented and I, unfortunately, didn't have one. When I first started as a federal vendor, I sort of just jump right into it. I was equipped with enough knowledge to get the ball going so I figured I would just wing it along the way.

Word of advice – DON'T WING IT.

Well, I followed all of the steps and was awarded my first federal contract within weeks of starting. I was super excited! However, in all my researching and communicating back and forth with the purchasing agency, I forgot to plan out the steps for fulfilling the order. I was responsible for buying the products they requested (with funding I'd secured) and then wait to be reimbursed by the agency. The problem was I hadn't done that so I ended up scrambling for small business loans and other funding. I was turned down mostly because my business was less than two years old. There were alternative funding options available but I had built any of those relationships yet. As a result of not having a detailed plan that covered multiple areas and scenarios as related to my business, I had to back out of my first awarded contract.

If you would look up, say about seventeen lines, there's a singled out sentence in bold lettering. I'll give you a moment to find it. See it? Yes? Great! Now let's repeat it together: **DON'T WING IT**.

Once you've set out to do THAT thing, you should now be intentional about everything you do when it comes to whatever that thing is. You have sought advice, you've done your due diligence, and you've dotted your I's and crossed your T's. In all your doing, if you haven't created or adopted a plan that has proven successful you have done yourself a great injustice. For example, if you're considering returning to college, an academic plan will lend to your successful completion. It will clearly outline courses for which you've already earned credits, whether or not those credits are transferable, and which courses you'll need to take to complete the degree/program you are pursuing. If you're hosting an event, you will need to outline your event goals and objectives then create a plan so that it all comes together.

D.R.E.AM Essential #3
Effective Systems

Here you are – ready to *do THAT thing*. You're excited and have pretty much figured out what you need to get started. So you start and you're off and running. You're making purchases and investments in support of your dream. You're making connections at networking events and social engagements. Calls are made and appointments are set. You are working it! Or are you?

From the very beginning, it is wise to utilize a system of tracking your every move. Be a little neurotic with it if you'd like. Color code receipts with different colored highlighters. Use sticky notes or a planner. Use whatever works for you but be sure to have a system. Lacking a system was one of my biggest mistakes. When I started my first business, I had no system – none whatsoever! I had contracted with a company to provide virtual customer service. I worked from home and set my own schedule. Sweet, huh? It was pretty sweet until started to feel like a hamster on a wheel. I couldn't remember what hours I was set to log in and serve customers. (But I'd create my OWN schedule, remember?) When I needed to provide legal documents to either open a bank account or as requested by the company I contracted with, I had to look through this folder or that folder. If what I was looking for wasn't there, then I'd look through the small stack of papers on my desk or through the bigger stack on the floor next to the desk. I was "organized" or so I thought. I figured that if I can put my hands on what I needed eventually, even if robbed me of time I could have used doing something productive, I was good. And why? Was it because I thought my "organized chaos" was cute? Was I glutton for punishment? I don't think so. I just didn't realize the importance of having an effective system in place.

Technology has made getting organized (and staying organized) simple. You should have no problem finding a system that would accommodate the things you've set out to do and the style of organizing you prefer. If you're anything like me, stuck between keeping a hard copy of EVERYTHING and utilizing the infamous "cloud", you have file folders, flash drives, and a virtual storage space. It really doesn't take all of that but I'm still a work in progress. I'm working to simplify my system by better utilizing some of the many apps and/or software options available. And you can too! More than likely, you have a smartphone. With a smartphone, it seems as though the possibilities for maintaining an effective system are endless. Right from your phone, you can schedule appointments, send and receive emails, and set event reminders.

There is a system out there for just about anything you want to do. Do you want to train to run your first 5K or marathon? There is a system built into a smartphone app that you can use to train for endurance. I've used one myself. (And just so you know, it was NOT for marathon training…lol!) One of my favorite applications is an all-in-one system built specifically with entrepreneurs in mind. It is beautifully designed (which really caught my eye) and has a lot of great features. You can manage your books, keep track of contacts, and schedule your calendar. There is even has an option that allows you to create and send client invoices. Now that's efficiency at its best! That is what I was looking for – a way to be more efficient – and that is what I found. You may be looking for a way to become more efficient or more productive. On the other hand, you may want to become more financially fit or more physically fit. No matter what you are looking to achieve, identify a system that has been tried and tested and go for it. Put the system in place and make it work for you. The key, however, is to maintain consistency in utilizing your system(s). It does not matter if you employ the best system ever made or the most expensive system you can buy. If you not consistent in using it to achieve the goal for which you implemented it, then it was just a waste of time.

D.R.E.A.M Essential #4
Accountability Partnership

Your mission has begun. You've set out on the road to *do THAT thing*. We have already talked about not going it alone. You will need someone to challenge you and hold you accountable once you put your goals out into the atmosphere. This is what an accountability partnership will do for you.

I used to think, *"Who would be more accountable than me in making sure I reach my goals?"* I realize I felt that way because I did not know the benefits of an accountability partnership. There are, in fact, many benefits. Personally, I have found that have an accountability partner keeps you focused. There will always be something (or someone) that will distract you from your goals. When it happens, you can easily get thrown off track. Having an accountability partnership can help ward off those distractions. Here are a few more benefits of an accountability partnership:

1. **An accountability partnership will help you measure your progress** – As you set out to *do THAT thing*, you have an idea of what success looks like to you. You may have even laid out a plan with milestones identified along the way.

2. **An accountability partnership will send your performance into overdrive** – You have someone to help you create a strategy designed with your success in mind. A sure-fire plan can do wonders for your confidence, sending your performance into a state of heightened activity.

3. **An accountability partnership will silence your inner critic** – As I mentioned earlier, some of us are so hard on ourselves. Nothing will be perfect and you have to come

to terms with that. Instead of becoming overwhelmed, discuss your concerns with your accountability partner. You will have someone with whom you can juggle ideas to help you make a sound decision. In addition, your accountability partner can offer constructive advice that will further encourage you.

D.R.E.A.M Essential #5
Management of Your Time

Time management, in my opinion, is an art form. I mean, consider everything you have to do in a normal day – wake up and get yourself (and your family, if applicable) going; breakfast; commuting; contribute to your career (either as an employer or as an employee); commuting; dinner; and wind down. That's an average day. But if you're anything like me, your typical day is more like this –

- early morning wakeup and quiet time with God
- coffee
- a little market research
- get son up and off to school
- back home for breakfast
- check emails
- social media networking
- play with grandbaby
- update blog posts and websites
- make phone calls
- work on client projects
- play with grandbaby again (he's so cute!)
- work on personal projects
- cook dinner
- do a load of laundry
- pick son up from one of his several team practices (he plays football, basketball, and has recently added track to list)
- dinner
- spend more time with the grandbaby (did I mention how cute he is?)
- wind down time
- lights out

Whoa!

In addition, I support my friends and loved ones by visiting them, joining them for a meal, and/or attending their events. I attend church, community events, school events, football games, and basketball games. I even make time for my significant other. Just how do I do it all? Is it magic? Nope. Here's how – time management. That's the key.

We all have the same twenty-four hours in a day. You can use them wisely or you can do like I used to do – sporadically jump from one project to the next with no real plan for how I would spend my day. At the beginning of this book, I talked about doing "stuff". I have to admit that I wasted a lot of time. At one time, I felt like I was just going in circles. I wanted desperately to get my act together. That's when learned a thing or two about efficiency. I sought advice from people who I thought had their stuff together. I asked what they were doing to accomplish everything they had to do within a day. Here's the advice I received that helped me become more efficient –

1. **Use a planner** – My pastor gave me this one. Get one and keep it with you. Schedule your entire day out and set a start time and end time for everything. For instance, let's look back at all of the things I do in a typical day. Let's say I schedule my time to check emails from 10:00am-10:30am. At 10 o'clock, that is what I'm working on. I read and respond to as many as I can until 10:30. At 10:30am, I'm done and I'm on to the next task. Trust me. It takes discipline but you can do it.

2. **Start early** – If you have to get up an hour earlier than usual so you can add more time to your day, do

it. I do. My day starts really early, usually around 5:00am. By the time I get my son up for school, I've usually already done a little research for my business or for a client and have designed a post for my social networking sites.

3. **Categorize your daily tasks** – You can decide how you would like to do this. One system that has been effective for me is categorizing tasks by levels –

   - A-level tasks: things that are a priority and must be done on that day. Some examples of A-level tasks are turning in your research paper due that day or a client coaching call schedule for that day.
   - B-level tasks: things that should be done today but if they aren't, they become a priority for the next day. An example is of a B-level task is comparing funding option for going back to college.
   - C-level tasks: things that, if you do them or not, have no negative affect on your ability to *do THAT thing*.
   - D-level tasks: things you can delegate to someone else so you can have more time to focus on the other tasks.

4. **Do the important things first** – There are going to be some things that you *have* to do but just don't *want* to do. These are often the things we tend to easily blow off. Tackle them first. Go on and get them out of the

way. Once you are done, you will no longer have them hanging over your head.

As I come to the close, there is something I would like to share – a moment of transparency. Throughout your reading, I have been giving you a glimpse into my life and my various lessons learned but here's one thing I did not mentioned that I need to do so right now.

I am not a finished product.

Every day, I strive to be better than the day before. Every day, I apply each of the principles I discuss in this book. In chapter one I urge you to **TRUST YOURSELF**. Well, guess what? I encourage myself too, on a daily basis, to trust myself and to be unstoppable. Personally, I make a conscious effort EVERY DAY to not entertain doubt and to speak positively. Is it always easy to do this every day? No. There have been times when I've wanted to throw in the towel, even while writing this book. I didn't though. I didn't give up. I followed the tips I've given you and I kept it moving. When I tell you to **BE ORIGINAL – BUT DON'T REINVENT THE WHEEL**, I follow my own advice as well. I am creative and always have been. Like me, you have to know, without a shadow of a doubt, that your visions can be thought-provoking and can bring about fresh ideas. My business is not original but there's something about it that makes it stand out. My story is not original but only I tell it like no one else can. And remember me telling you "**DON'T GO IT ALONE**". That's great advice too. How do I know? I started my journey that way – alone. At one time in my life, I had some serious trust issues – with friends, with family, with just about everyone. And I tell you, it could get pretty lonely being alone.

Even if you have to do what I did – convince myself that I had too much to offer to be alone – make sure you have the support of those who love you and have your best interest at heart. Most importantly, **BELIEVE IN YOU**. Equipped with these principles and your D.R.E.A.M Roadmap, you are bound to have success as you *do THAT thing*.